This book is dedicated to my partner Natasha and our three beautiful daughters.

I also give thanks and respect to all of my family, the descendants of Albert Namatjira. I'm so proud that we're carrying on his legacy.

And to our next generations, may you write your own stories, and make your own history.

ALBERT NAMATJIRA
BY VINCENT NAMATJIRA

My name is Vincent Namatjira.

I want to tell you the story of my great-grandfather Albert Namatjira – one of Australia's most important artists.

Albert was a Western Aranda man from Ntaria (Hermannsburg). He grew up on the Lutheran mission there.

01
01

Albert showed early promise as an artist and craftsman. He made traditional artefacts, like boomerangs, which he also painted. He sold these artefacts to people working in Ntaria or passing through, like policemen.

Albert first learned about landscape painting from a man named Rex Battarbee, an artist from Melbourne who was visiting Central Australia. Albert showed Rex beautiful places to paint and taught him about his Country. In return Rex taught Albert about watercolour painting. Despite their different backgrounds, Albert and Rex became close friends.

Albert had a special talent for painting. He was able to capture the unique light and the beauty of his Country. His first ever exhibition in Melbourne was a sell-out. Albert also had sell-out exhibitions in Sydney and Adelaide. The people living in those cities at the time wouldn't have known very much about Aboriginal people living in the outback, but they loved Albert's paintings.

Albert's success as an artist brought him fame and money. He could afford nice clothes and cars, and he travelled to different cities for exhibitions. Albert was so successful that even the Queen took notice of what he was doing. Albert met the Queen and received a Coronation Medal, which must have been a strange experience for a bloke from the bush.

At the height of his fame, Albert had his portrait painted by another artist named William Dargie. Dargie's portrait of Albert won the 1956 Archibald Prize. This was recognition of Dargie's skill but also of Albert's respected position in the art world.

When Albert was away travelling,

he always missed his home.

He really just wanted to be back

living a simple life on his Country

with his family.

Albert became the first Aboriginal person to be made an Australian citizen. At this time, Aboriginal people weren't considered citizens of Australia even though they had been living on their Country for thousands of years. Albert was a proud representative for his people, but it must have been a strange and complicated time for him.

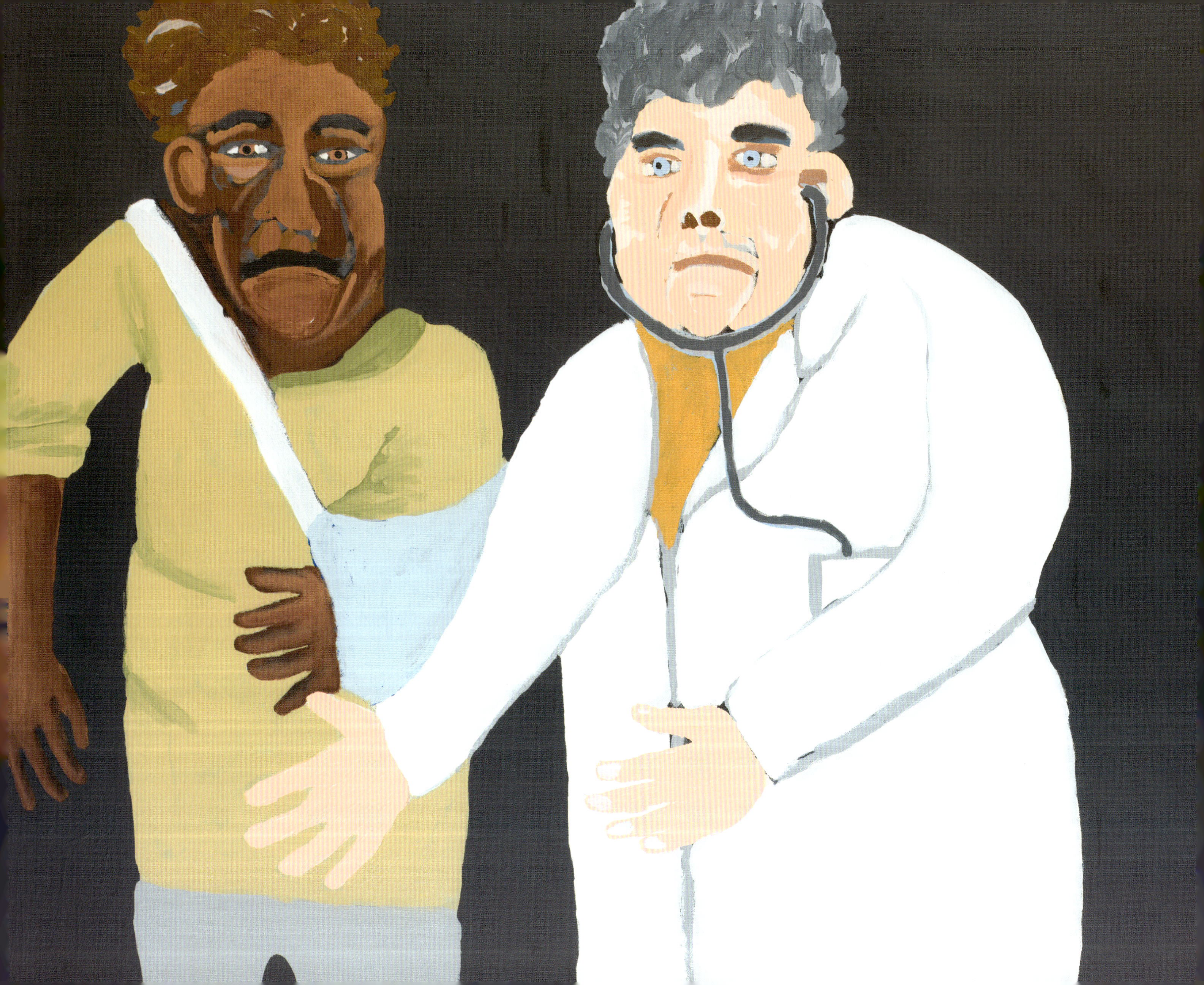

Back in Alice Springs, Albert hurt himself when he was working on his car and the bonnet fell down on his hand. An artist's hands are their most important tools, so Albert must have felt sad. This was the beginning of a lot of problems for Albert and a difficult time.

As an Australian citizen, Albert was allowed to vote, buy land, build a house, and to buy alcohol. Although it was legal for Albert to buy alcohol, it was against the law for him to supply or share it with other Aboriginal people, like his family and friends. This eventually got Albert in trouble with the law.

Albert was sentenced to prison for supplying an Aboriginal person with liquor. He was sad and ashamed. He had been living in two very different worlds – one as a famous, successful artist, and one as a Western Aranda man with cultural and family responsibilities. He must have felt weary from trying to balance these two cultures, and he became unwell.

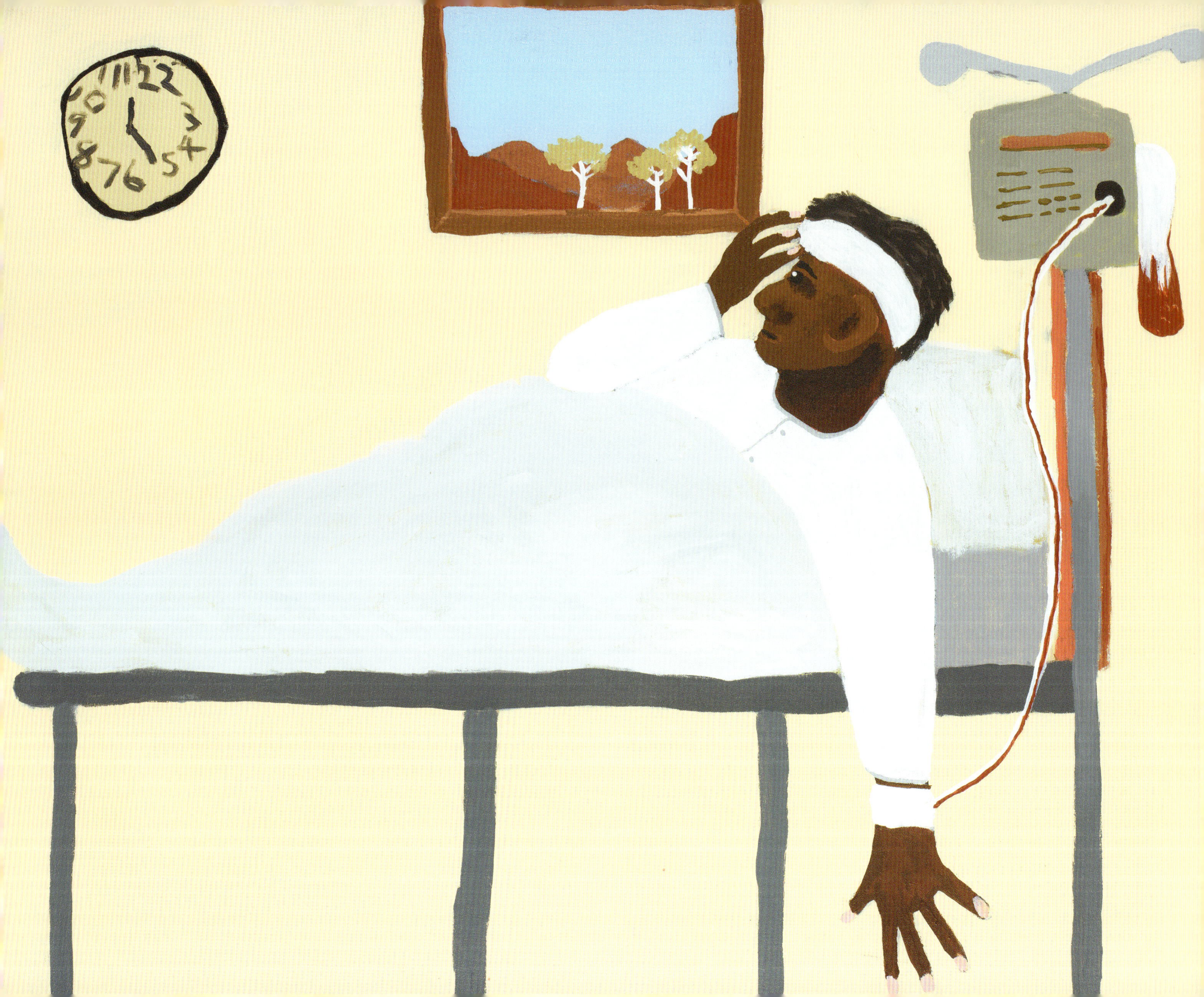

Albert was getting older and feeling very tired. He lived a full life and achieved many great things, despite all the challenges faced by Aboriginal people at the time. Albert passed away in Alice Springs Hospital. Some say he died of a broken heart. I just hope when he was in hospital he had a window so he could see out to the Country he painted so beautifully.

Albert Namatjira changed the face of art in Australia, and was the first Aboriginal man to really be noticed and acknowledged by non-Indigenous Australians. Despite facing hardships and injustice, Albert left behind an amazing legacy. The paintings he made of his beloved Country are in important galleries and museums and they continue to make an impact on the people who see them.

ABOUT ALBERT NAMATJIRA

1902 Born Ntaria (Hermannsburg), Northern Territory

1936 Meets Rex Battarbee and makes first watercolour paintings

1938 First solo exhibition in Melbourne, Victoria

1944 Included in *Who's Who in Australia*

1953 Receives the Coronation Medal

1954 Meets Queen Elizabeth II in Canberra, Australian Capital Territory

1955 Elected an Honorary Member of the Royal Art Society of New South Wales

1957 First Indigenous person to be granted Australian citizenship

1959 Died Alice Springs, Northern Territory

ABOUT VINCENT NAMATJIRA

1983 Born Mparntwe (Alice Springs), Northern Territory

2013 Paints first figurative portraits at Iwantja art centre, Indulkana Community, South Australia

2014 British Museum, London, acquires the Vincent Namatjira painting *James Cook – with the Declaration*

2018 First Indigenous Australian artist to present a solo exhibition at Art Basel, Miami Beach, Florida

2019 Wins RAMSAY Art Prize at the Art Gallery of South Australia

2020 Receives the Medal of the Order of Australia (OAM) for services to Indigenous art and the community

2020 First Indigenous winner of the Archibald Prize

Acknowledgements

Vincent Namatjira would like to thank:

Beth Conway and Heath Aarons at Iwantja Arts; Iltja Ntjarra (Many Hands) Art Centre; Hermannsburg Potters; Dianne Tanzer and Nicola Stein at THIS IS NO FANTASY, Melbourne; Bruce Johnson McLean; Queensland Art Gallery | Gallery of Modern Art (QAGOMA); Magabala Books; Maryann Ballantyne; and friends and family.

Magabala Books would like to thank:

The Queensland Art Gallery / Gallery of Modern Art (QAGOMA) and Iwantja Arts for their support in producing this book.

NOTE TO THE READER

The author has used 'Aranda' throughout as the preferred spelling for the language group (Western Aranda) of Albert Namatjira and Vincent Namatjira and recognises that there are other spellings (for example, Arrernte, Arranta and Arranda) but this is the preferred spelling agreed on by the majority of artists descended from Albert Namatjira. The author thanks Iltja Ntjarra (Many Hands) Art Centre for its guidance on this.

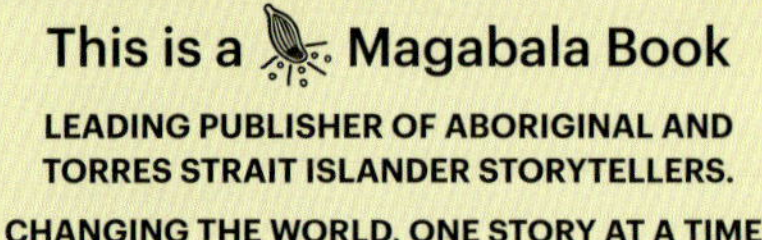

First published 2021, reprinted 2022 and 2025
Magabala Books Aboriginal Corporation, Broome, Western Australia
Website: www.magabala.com Email: sales@magabala.com

Magabala Books receives financial assistance from the Commonwealth Government through the Australia Council, its arts advisory body. The State of Western Australia has made an investment in this project through the Department of Local Government, Sport and Cultural Industries.

Magabala Books is Australia's only independent Aboriginal and Torres Strait Islander publishing house. Magabala Books acknowledges the Traditional Owners of the Country on which we live and work. We recognise the unbroken connection to traditional lands, waters and cultures. Through what we publish, we honour all our Elders, peoples and stories, past, present and future.

Printed in China by Everbest Printing Co. Ltd.
Consultant Editor: Heath Aarons
Packaged by Ballantyne Rawlins in collaboration with Magabala Books.

The artworks in this book were created using acrylic on canvas, the cover image is acrylic on paper, and the portraits accompanying the artists' biographies are lithographic prints.

All artworks are part of the Indigenous Australian Art Collection: Namatjira Story, Queensland Art Gallery | Gallery of Modern Art (QAGOMA) with the exception of the cover, page 4, page 28, page 30 and page 31, courtesy of the artist, Iwantja Arts and THIS IS NO FANTASY.

ISBN 978-1-925936-21-6 (Print)
ISBN 978-1-925936-22-3 (ePDF)

A catalogue record for this book is available from the National Library of Australia

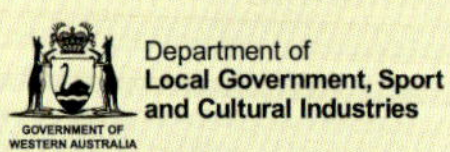

Iwantja Arts

Iwantja Arts is an Indigenous owned and governed Aboriginal art centre, located in the rocky, desert country of the Indulkana Community on the Aṉangu Pitjantjatjara Yankunytjatjara (APY) Lands in the remote north-west of South Australia. Iwantja Arts is named after the Iwantja Creek near where the Indulkana Community was founded, which is the site of the Tjurki (native owl) Tjukurpa.

Iwantja Arts supports the artistic careers of its more than 40 predominantly Yankunytjatjara artist members, providing access to artistic and professional development. Iwantja Arts is renowned for its innovative and culturally rich projects with prestigious outcomes that celebrate Aṉangu cultural strength and artistic excellence.

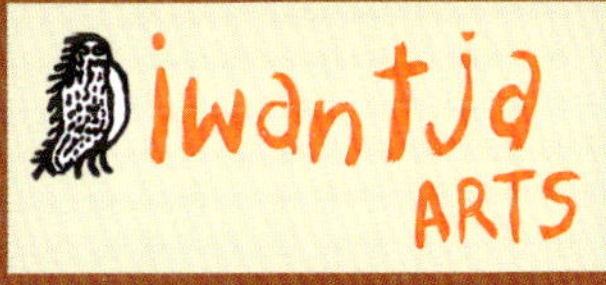